CHRISTMAS AROUND THE WORLD

Now when Jesus was born in Bethlehem of Judea
in the days of Herod the king, behold, wise men from the East
came to Jerusalem, saying,
"Where is he who has been born king of the Jews?
For we have seen his star in the East,
and have come to worship him."

Matthew 2:1-2

CHRISTMAS IN THE HOLY LAND

CHRISTMAS AROUND THE WORLD
FROM WORLD BOOK

World Book, Inc.
a Scott Fetzer company
Chicago

Bible passages quoted in *Christmas in the Holy Land*
are from THE HOLY BIBLE, Revised Standard
Version, an ecumenical edition.

CHRISTMAS IN THE HOLY LAND was prepared by the
Editorial and Art Departments of World Book, Inc.

Copyright © 1987 by World Book, Inc.
525 W. Monroe
Chicago, IL 60661

**For information on other World Book products,
call 1-800-255-1750, x. 2238, or visit us at
our Web site at http://www.worldbook.com**

Printed in Singapore

ISBN: 0-7166-0887-1
Library of Congress Catalog Card No. 87-50393

6 7 8 9 10 99 98

CONTENTS

THE NATIVITY

Detail of *Adoration of Magi* by Bassano (workshop)
About 1550. Pinacoteca, Sansepolcros, Italy

Detail of *Prophet Isaiah* by Michaelangelo
1512. Sistine Chapel, Vatican, Rome

or to us a child is born,
to us a son is given; and
the government will be upon
his shoulder,
and his name will be called "Wonderful
Counselor, Mighty God, Everlasting Father,
Prince of Peace."

Isaiah 9: 6

9

Tree of Jesse by unknown craftsman
About 1220. Stained glass window from Cathedral of Autun
St. Lazare, France

The book of the genealogy of Jesus Christ, the son of David, the son of Abraham.

Abraham was the father of Isaac, and Isaac the father of Jacob, and Jacob the father of Judah and his brothers,

and Judah the father of Perez and Zerah by Tamar, and Perez the father of Hezron, and Hezron the father of Ram,

and Ram the father of Amminadab, and Amminadab the father of Nahshon, and Nahshon the father of Salmon,

and Salmon the father of Boaz by Rahab, and Boaz the father of Obed by Ruth, and Obed the father of Jesse,

and Jesse the father of David the king. And David was the father of Solomon by the wife of Uriah,

and Solomon the father of Rehoboam, and
Rehoboam the father of Abijah, and Abijah
the father of Asa,
and Asa the father of Jehoshaphat, and
Jehoshaphat the father of Joram, and Joram
the father of Uzziah,
and Uzziah the father of Jotham, and Jotham
the father of Ahaz, and Ahaz the father of
Hezekiah,
and Hezekiah the father of Manasseh, and
Manasseh the father of Amos, and Amos the
father of Josiah,
and Josiah the father of Jechoniah and his
brothers, at the time of the deportation to
Babylon.
And after the deportation to Babylon:
Jechoniah was the father of Shealtiel, and
Shealtiel the father of Zerubbabel,
and Zerubbabel the father of Abiud, and

Abiud the father of Eliakim, and Eliakim the father of Azor,

and Azor the father of Zadok, and Zadok the father of Achim, and Achim the father of Eliud,

and Eliud the father of Eleazar, and Eleazar the father of Matthan, and Matthan the father of Jacob,

and Jacob the father of Joseph the husband of Mary, of whom Jesus was born, who is called Christ.

So all the generations from Abraham to David were fourteen generations, and from David to the deportation to Babylon fourteen generations, and from the deportation to Babylon to the Christ fourteen generations.

Matthew 1: 1-17

David
by Verrocchio
About 1470. Bargello, Florence

J esus, through Joseph descended from David, legendary King of Israel. Jesus, through David, descended from Abraham, the patriarch to whom God revealed His presence and through whom God formed His covenant with man. Between Jesus and the Jewish exile in Babylon, there were fourteen generations. Between the exile and David, there were fourteen generations. Between David and Abraham, there were fourteen generations.

Matthew thus begins his story of the birth of Christ. Of what significance is this genealogy? What does it mean to us, nearly 2,000 years later?

Through Abraham, Jehovah, the one God, made His presence known to man, and through Abraham, the Lord formed a covenant with the people of Israel:

> *On that day the LORD made a*
> *covenant with Abram, saying, "To*
> *your descendants I give this land,*
> *from the river of Egypt to the great*
> *river, the river Euphrates. . .*
>
> Genesis 15: 18

With David, the Lord entered into another covenant. If David would build a house of God, his descendants would forever rule over the land from the river of Egypt to the river Euphrates:

> *He shall build a house for my name,*
> *and I will establish the throne of his*
> *kingdom for ever.*
>
> II Samuel 7: 13

In either the year 587 or 586 B.C., Babylonians, under King Nebuchadnezzar, conquered Judah, toppled the dynasty founded by David, and destroyed the Temple of Solomon, the house of God. The leaders of Israel were forced into exile in Babylonia. Before and during the time of the Babylonian captivity, prophets rose up and warned the people of Israel that it was they, not God, who broke the covenant. The prophets also foretold of a Messiah who would lead the people back to righteousness. And this Messiah would be of the house of David:

> *"Behold, the days are coming, says*
> *the LORD, when I will fulfil the*
> *promise I made to the house of Israel*
> *and the house of Judah. In those days*
> *and at that time I will cause a*
> *righteous Branch to spring forth for*
> *David; and he shall execute justice*
> *and righteousness in the land. . ."*
>
> Jeremiah 33: 14-15

The Babylonian exile came to an end when a Persian, Cyrus, conquered Babylonia. Cyrus allowed the captured Jews to return to Judah. He did not, however, restore David's line to the throne. Israel was still a captive state. After Cyrus, the land between the river of Egypt and the great river Euphrates was held first by Alexander the

Great of Macedonia, then by the Ptolemies of Egypt, by the Seleucids of Syria, and in the time of Jesus, by the Caesars of Rome. The past was not, however, forgotten.

The glory of the reigns of David and of Solomon was told and retold. The history of Israel was preserved in the Books, which have come down to us as the Old Testament. Generation after generation of Jews learned of their own past and learned of the prophecies. The Lord had promised. There would be a Messiah who would lead the people back into the ways of righteousness. And with this, the Lord's covenants with Abraham and David would be restored.

Matthew begins the telling of the story of the birth of Christ, the Greek word for Messiah, with a genealogy that proves to the reader that Jesus, a descendant of David, was the beginning of the fulfillment of the prophecies and of the Lord's promise. Matthew completes the telling of the generations of Jesus with a counting: there were between Abraham and David fourteen generations; there were between David and Solomon and the exile fourteen generations; there were between the exile and Jesus fourteen generations. There is an elegant symmetry to this. But what is the significance?

The patriarch of Israel was Abraham. It began with him; with God's revelation to him; and His covenant with him. In fourteen generations, the promise to the people of Israel reached its zenith in the reigns of David and Solomon. In fourteen days, a new moon reaches its zenith as a full moon. In another fourteen generations, the zenith reached in the time of David waned into the catastrophe of exile in Babylon. In fourteen days, the full moon wanes into a setting moon. Fourteen generations after the exile, Jesus, the Christ, was born. The period of the full moon had, with Him, come round again. The fourteen generations correspond to the fourteen days of lunar waxing and waning. Matthew compares the waxing and waning of the glory of Israel to the cycles of the moon. Matthew's comparison is, however, more than just a comparison; it teaches a lesson. There is an elegant symmetry to all things. There is order to all things because it is all God's plan, His work. It is *all* one thing.

The Rock of Abraham has, since Biblical times, been identified as the place where Abraham prepared to sacrifice his son Isaac. On this Rock, David placed the Ark of the Covenant. Around this Rock, Solomon built the first Temple, and Herod the Great built the third Temple, where Jesus worshiped. Held sacred by Muslims, as well as by Jews and Christians, the Rock of Abraham is, according to Muslim belief, the place where the blessed enter Paradise. The Dome of the Rock, a Muslim shrine, was built over the Rock in A.D. 687.

Detail of *Annunciation* by Botticelli
1489-1490. Uffizi, Florence, Italy

n the sixth month the angel Gabriel was sent from God to a city of Galilee named Nazareth, to a virgin betrothed to a man whose name was Joseph, of the house of David; and the virgin's name was Mary.

And he came to her and said, "Hail, O favored one, the Lord is with you!"

But she was greatly troubled at the saying, and considered in her mind what sort of greeting this might be.

And the angel said to her, "Do not be afraid, Mary, for you have found favor with God.

And behold, you will conceive in your womb and bear a son, and you shall call his name Jesus.

He will be great, and will be called
the Son of the Most High;
and the Lord God will give to him
the throne of his father David,

and he will reign over the house of

    Jacob for ever;

and of his kingdom there will be no

    end."

And Mary said to the angel, "How shall this be,

since I have no husband?"

And the angel said to her,

    "The Holy Spirit will come upon

        you,

    and the power of the Most High will

        overshadow you;

    therefore the child to be born will be

        called holy,

    the Son of God. . ."

Luke 1: 26-35

In the days of Herod the Great, King of Judea, an angel of the Lord appeared to a young maiden by the name of Mary. Little is known of this woman who all later generations have called blessed among women. She lived in Nazareth, a tiny and insignificant village close to a major trade route to and from Egypt. Although ancient, this town was, until the time of Mary and Joseph, of so little consequence that it is not mentioned in any of the books of the Old Testament. She was, when the angel appeared before her, betrothed, that is, formally engaged, to a man named Joseph. The couple was legally bound in marriage, but the final vows had not been completed. She was a virgin.

Luke identifies the angel who appeared to Mary as Gabriel, the same angel who appeared to Zechariah and, generations before, to Daniel. In the time of the Babylonian exile, Daniel lived as a member of the royal court of first Nebuchadnezzar and then Belshazzar. Gifted, Daniel interpreted dreams and other portents for the Babylonian kings. It was Daniel who explained to Belshazzar the meaning of the "handwriting on the wall." It was Daniel who, when thrown into the lion's den, survived through his absolute faith in the Lord. And it was Daniel who, unable to understand one of his own dreams, heard the voice of God in address to His angel: "Gabriel, make this man understand the vision." Gabriel is, thus, introduced as an interpreter of God.

And, thus, it was Gabriel who was sent to announce the conception of the Christ and to interpret for Mary the meaning of this conception, the meaning of the plan: "Hail, O favored one, the Lord is with you." Mary, upon seeing the angel, is described as "greatly troubled." She became thoughtful, wondering what this vision could mean. When Daniel saw the angel, he was "frightened and fell upon his face." While Daniel, an adviser to kings, a man who faced a den of lions, was frightened to the point of collapse, Mary, an innocent girl, was merely troubled. The comparison in reactions tells much about this woman and much about why she found "favor with God."

Mary was courageous. A young woman who is pregnant, pregnant with a child that is not her husband's, needs courage. But many before and many after Mary have faced this ordeal. This woman was unique; she was to be the mother of the Messiah. And the mother of the Messiah must find within herself great courage indeed.

Mary was thoughtful. The mother of the Christ must be thoughtful, for her Son is like no other; her Son will not behave as others behave; her Son will not think as others think. This is a thing she must understand. The force of the will of God is a thing she must understand, a thing she must accept.

> And behold, you will conceive in your womb
>   and bear a son,
> And you shall call his name Jesus.

You shall call his name Jesus—God is salvation; for it is Jesus who will reveal the salvation of God. So the plan is revealed to the Mother, and she questions it but once: "How shall this be, since I have no husband?" Through Gabriel, the Lord replies: "For with God nothing is impossible." And Mary, the woman of faith, accepts His plan, as well as her own fate: "Behold, I am the handmaid of the Lord; let it be to me according to your word."

It is not recorded that Mary ever again questioned her fate. It is not recorded that she ever again questioned God's will or any single link of that chain of events that began with her in that once unknown place and which led, inevitably, to another place, the place known as Golgotha.

Detail (Joseph) of *Mérode Altarpiece* by Robert Campin
About 1425. Metropolitan Museum of Art,
The Cloister Collection, New York City

ow the birth of Jesus
Christ took place in this way.

When his mother Mary had been betrothed to
Joseph, before they came together she was
found to be with child of the Holy Spirit;
and her husband Joseph, being a just man and
unwilling to put her to shame, resolved to
divorce her quietly.

But as he considered this, behold, an angel of
the Lord appeared to him in a dream, saying,
"Joseph, son of David, do not fear to take Mary
your wife, for that which is conceived in her is
of the Holy Spirit;
she will bear a son, and you shall call his name
Jesus, for he will save his people from their
sins."

Matthew 1: 18-21

M ary, a young woman living in Nazareth, was betrothed, that is, formally engaged, to a man named Joseph, who was of the line of David. In those days, betrothal, under Jewish law, was a legal contract, binding as marriage. A man betrothed to a woman called her his wife; she called him her husband. If a betrothed husband died before the marriage vows were completed, the woman was legally his widow. A betrothal could be broken, but only by divorce. This was, however, an option open only to men.

Before Mary and Joseph completed the vows of marriage, she informed him that she was with child. This was grounds for divorce. Joseph had two options: he could publicly expose her condition by bringing her before the court; or he could divorce her discreetly by handing her a writ in the presence of two witnesses.

> *and her husband Joseph, being a just*
> *man and unwilling to put her to*
> *shame, resolved to divorce her quietly.*

Joseph is described as a just man, that is, a man who observed the laws of Abraham and Moses. As a man who observed the laws, he was also a man of faith. As a man of faith, a man of wisdom and kindness, he chose a course of discretion. He would divorce Mary as quietly as possible. He would not hold her up to public shame.

Beyond this display of discretion, we know very little of this man, Joseph. We know he was of the line of David, and as a descendant of David, we know his ancestral home was Bethlehem. Joseph, however, chose to live in Nazareth. We do not know why.

We know Joseph was a carpenter. Although Joseph's profession is never mentioned in the New Testament, Jesus is identified as the "son of the carpenter." This was a valued skill in a country almost entirely devoted to agriculture. Carpenters made the tools needed to till the land: plows, threshing boards, yokes, and other implements. Carpenters of the day made furniture: tables and benches and beds. And they made coffins. Joseph's tools would have been the same tools described, generations before, by Isaiah, the prophet: the compass, pencil, plane, saw, hammer, axe, adz, chisel, plumb line, drill, file, and square. Joseph would have learned his trade from his father, and he would have passed on his skills to his sons, as was the custom. In Mark, Jesus himself is identified as "the carpenter."

We know that Joseph was a man of faith. Before serving Mary with a writ of divorcement, he had a dream. In the dream, an angel of the Lord appeared to him and informed him that Mary's unborn child was conceived "of the Holy Spirit," that the Child was to be a Son, and that His name was to be Jesus—God is salvation.

God's plan was, thus, revealed to Joseph. As a man of faith, he could neither ignore nor misunderstand that plan. Like any man descended from a king, especially a very great king, Joseph must have been very aware of his ancestry. As a "just man" Joseph must also have been aware of the ancient prophecies:

> *In those days and at that time I will*
> *cause a righteous Branch to spring*
> *forth for David;*
> *and he shall execute justice and*
> *righteousness in the land.*

Jeremiah 33: 15

In the dream, the angel identifies Joseph through David: "Joseph, son of David, do not fear to take Mary your wife." Knowing the prophecies, the just man did as he was commanded. He accepted the dream, the Lord's command, as an article of faith; he took Mary as his wife. Through Joseph, the ancient prophecies were fulfilled. And Joseph, like Mary, became a vessel through whom a righteous Branch sprang forth for David, through whom justice and righteousness were executed in the land.

*Primarily Muslim, **Nazareth** does draw Christian pilgrims to such sites as Mary's Well, an ancient well from which people still draw water, and the Latin Church of the Annunciation, the traditional site of the home of Mary, Mother of Jesus.*

Detail of *Joseph and Mary in Bethlehem*
by unknown artist (Flemish school)
About 1560. Scaiffe Gallery, Pittsburgh, Pennsylvania

In those days a decree went out from Caesar Augustus that all the world should be enrolled.
This was the first enrollment, when Quirinius was governor of Syria.
And all went to be enrolled, each to his own city.
And Joseph also went up from Galilee, from the city of Nazareth, to Judea, to the city of David, which is called Bethlehem, because he was of the house and lineage of David, to be enrolled with Mary, his betrothed, who was with child.

Luke 2: 1-5

Augustus Caesar
by unknown Roman sculptor
About A.D. 14-50.
Braccio Nuova, Rome

A decree went out from Caesar Augustus. In the year to which those words refer, the most powerful man on earth was Caesar Augustus, Emperor of all the Roman world. Born Gaius Octavius in 44 B.C., a great-nephew of the conqueror Julius Caesar, Octavius inherited the mantle of Caesar, vanquished his foes, and became Augustus the Emperor.

Rome's dominion extended from the English Channel across Western Europe, through the Mediterranean world, and well into Asia. Augustus himself was responsible for the restoration of peace and order after nearly a century of civil war. His reign as emperor marked the establishment of the *Pax Romana,* a 200-year period of relative peace throughout the civilized world. Peace it was, but a peace enforced by the iron might of Roman armies. Along with peace, Augustus brought prosperity. He was said to have found Rome brick and left it marble. So it was, under the rule of Augustus, that the very name of Rome came to mean power, authority, and wealth.

In a corner of a conquered province of the mighty Roman Empire, a poor and obscure couple, Mary and Joseph, journeyed from their home in the north to the little town of Bethlehem, in the south. They traveled because the decree of Caesar Augustus ordered "all the world," that is, all of the peoples of the Roman Empire, to be enrolled, or counted, in their hometowns and villages, for the purpose of taxation.

Joseph was of the house of David. So they returned to the birthplace of David—Bethlehem.

The name Bethlehem means "house of bread." The origin of the name is, most probably, a reflection of the town's favored location in an area that is relatively fertile. In the days of Caesar Augustus, fig and olive trees grew here. Men and women harvested fields of wheat and carried the grain into the little town, where it was ground and made into flour for bread. On the hills surrounding the town, shepherds kept watch over their flocks of sheep. It was a gentle kind of place in a land that was not, and is not, gentle.

Cut by the Great Rift Valley, the world's longest and deepest scar, the Holy Land is a region of awesome contrasts. It is possible, in a single day, to walk from such places as Bethlehem into the near-lunar landscape of the Wilderness of Judea, which, as one observer noted, produces a "sense of living next door to doom." And, perhaps, it was this extraordinary contrast that has, throughout time, triggered in man the contemplation of God and of man's place in relation to God; a contrast that triggered the endless searchings of holy men and the visions of prophets.

And according to the prophets, Bethlehem was more than a fertile place and more than the birthplace of David. It was *to be* the birthplace of the Messiah. For in Micah, it was written:

> *But you, O Bethlehem Ephrathah,*
> *who are little to be among the clans*
> *of Judah,*
> *from you shall come forth for me*
> *one who is to be ruler in Israel,*
> *whose origin is from of old,*
> *from ancient days.*
>
> Micah 5: 2

From you, insignificant Bethlehem, will come Him, the anointed one, the Messiah; and He will be descended from the ancient days of glory, from mighty King David.

And so on that night, some two thousand years ago, Joseph, a true descendant of David, traveled toward Bethlehem. And with Joseph traveled Mary, his wife, filled with child and filled with the knowledge of God's will, of His plan.

*Modern-day **Bethlehem,** built upon the site of ancient Bethlehem, is primarily a religious shrine. Containing a large number of churches and religious institutions sponsored by the Eastern Orthodox Church, the Roman Catholic Church, and Protestant faiths, the city lies about five miles south of Jerusalem, in the part of Jordan that has been occupied by Israel since 1967.*

Detail of *Nativity — Predella of Strozzi Altarpiece*
by Gentile da Fabriano
1423. Uffizi, Florence, Italy

And while they were there,
the time came for her to be
delivered.
And she gave birth to her first-born son
and wrapped him in swaddling cloths,
and laid him in a manger,
because there was no place for them in the
inn.

Luke 2: 6-7

Mary and Joseph journeyed, probably on foot, to Bethlehem, a little town not far from Jerusalem. And when they arrived, they found Bethlehem filled with others who had made similar trips, all because the mighty Caesar Augustus in faraway Rome had decreed that it be so. And, perhaps, knowing it was useless, Mary and Joseph went into the town's only inn and asked for a room. The proprietor, most probably tired and out-of-sorts from the extra work, shrugged his shoulders and said, "There is nothing. Can't you see the way things are?" Did Mary, then, sit in the deep shade found under the columned arcade around the market square while Joseph walked up and down the streets, knocking on doors, asking if he could rent a bed? Perhaps he was sent from one house to another: "Try down the street, she had an extra room this morning." And did a stranger, taking pity on Joseph, when he told her his wife was with child, offer them the use of the stable, which was, perhaps, in a cave behind the house?

Did Joseph, then, return to the square, to his wife, and say, "The only place I could find is in a stable"? She may have smiled as he helped her to her feet, smiled because the stable was better than nothing and because she knew her time was coming near. And when they got there, to the stable, did he help her lie down on a bed of straw?

Perhaps, then, he left her to go to the well to get water: water with which he washed her face and her hands and her feet; water with which he wiped her brow through the long hours of labor; water with which he washed the Baby when finally It came. And, then, did Joseph hand the Baby to Mary and did she hold Him to her breast until He fell asleep? And when the Baby was asleep, did she, then, whisper to her husband, "In the bundle, there is linen"? Joseph found the linen, which, perhaps, came with Mary as part of her dowry, and he began to tear along the warp, tear it into strips, which he handed to Mary. Then she began, as she had seen others do before her, to swaddle the Child, to carefully wrap Him to make Him feel secure, to make Him feel warm. When she was done, she placed the Child in the manger, into the bed of straw.

And did they, then, look into each other's eyes, look without speaking, for there was no need to speak? Each knew what the other was thinking. His name would be Joshua—Jesus—Salvation of God. It was Him. It did not matter that He was born in this place, for they knew. Months before, Mary and then Joseph had been told. They alone knew His plan. They knew the promise had been fulfilled.

The **Grotto of the Nativity** lies below the Church of the Nativity in Bethlehem. This cave was identified as the birthplace of Jesus by St. Helena, the mother of Constantine, first Christian emperor of Rome. He built a church over the grotto in A.D. 325. Sections of this structure remain, enclosed and built upon by the Emperor Justinian in A.D. 560. The actual spot of the Birth is marked with a silver star (left) inscribed: 'Hic de virgine Maria, Jesus christus natus est' (Here Jesus Christ was born of the Virgin Mary). Above the star is the altar of the Birth of Christ (above). On Christmas Eve, the Roman Catholic Patriarch of Jerusalem leads a procession to this altar for devotion and prayer.

Detail of *The Adoration of the Shepherds* by Giorgione
About 1506. National Gallery of Art, Washington, D.C.

And in that region there were shepherds out in the field, keeping watch over their flock by night. And an angel of the Lord appeared to them, and the glory of the Lord shone around them, and they were filled with fear. And the angel said to them, "Be not afraid; for behold, I bring you good news of a great joy which will come to all the people; for to you is born this day in the city of David a Savior, who is Christ the Lord. And this will be a sign for you: you will find a babe wrapped in swaddling cloths and lying in a manger." And suddenly there was with the angel a multitude of the heavenly host praising God and saying,

"Glory to God in the highest,
and on earth peace among men with
whom he is pleased!"

When the angels went away from them into
heaven, the shepherds said to one another,
"Let us go over to Bethlehem and see this
thing that has happened, which the Lord has
made known to us."
And they went with haste, and found Mary
and Joseph, and the babe lying in a manger.
And when they saw it they made known the
saying which had been told them concerning
this child;
and all who heard it wondered at what the
shepherds told them.
But Mary kept all these things, pondering
them in her heart.
And the shepherds returned, glorifying and
praising God for all they had heard and seen,
as it had been told them.

Luke 2: 8-20

There were, on the night Jesus was born, shepherds out in the fields around Bethlehem, keeping watch over their flocks. An angel of the Lord appeared unto these men, filling them with fear. And the angel said, "Do not be afraid. I am a messenger of the Lord, bringing the greatest possible news. Tonight, in Bethlehem, in the city of David, the long hoped-for Messiah, the Christ, has been born. You will find Him wrapped in swaddling clothes, lying in a manger. Go to Him."

The first to know of the birth of the Messiah were shepherds, simple men of low birth. The coming of the Christ was not announced to Herod in his palace. It was not told to the priests in the great Temple in Jerusalem. Caesar Augustus in faraway Rome knew nothing of the event. A great multitude of the heavenly host, all the angels of heaven, praising God and His work, appeared before the shepherds. Why was the birth of Jesus revealed to these men and to no one else?

In Judea in the time of Jesus, sheep were an important part of the life of the country. They were the chief sustenance and wealth of the Hebrew people. They provided meat, milk, wool, and skins. Sheep were also central to the elaborate rituals that were carried on daily in the

To this day, shepherds watch over their flocks of sheep on the hills surrounding Bethlehem.

Temple in Jerusalem. When the Lord spared Isaac, the son of Abraham, it was a ram that was substituted in sacrifice. And the sacrifice of sheep continued from the days of Abraham into the time of Jesus.

While sheep were central to the life of Israel, the shepherds who watched over them were not thought to be of much importance. Evidence indicates that sheep herding and shepherds in general were given little respect. An ancient rabbinical writing bluntly asserts: "the testimony of robbers, shepherds, violent men, and in fact all who are under suspicion when it comes to money, is invalid." Urban people must have viewed rural shepherds with great suspicion. They led rather lonely lives, spending long hours in endless watch over their flocks.

Shepherds did, however, have a proud heritage, for the great leaders of Israel had all been shepherds: Abraham, Moses, and, of course, David. The Books of the Bible are filled with both symbolic and literal references to the shepherd and his sheep. As the shepherds were to their sheep, so God was to His flock, the people of Israel. Again and again, this image is repeated. The man lost to God is like the sheep who wanders from the flock. Through the Books of the New Testament, Jesus is referred to and refers to himself as "the good shepherd," "the chief shepherd," who "lays down his life for the sheep." If the Messiah and ultimately God were the symbolic shepherds of mankind, then the real shepherds, the simple, the lowly, the humble, the men of expectant

Although no longer a primary means of transportation, herds of camels are still raised in the Holy Land.

A modern-day goatherd drives
his goats along a road near the
outskirts of Bethlehem.

hearts, were the Lord's flock. It was to them and for them that Jesus was
sent. And it was to them that His birth was announced:

> "Be not afraid; for behold, I bring
> you good news of a great joy which
> will come to all the people;
> for to you is born this day in the city
> of David a Savior, who is Christ the
> Lord. . ."

Great joy will come to *all* the people. For to *you*, the humble and the
expectant, is born a Savior.

And that night the shepherds left their flocks and went into
Bethlehem, and they found Mary and Joseph and the Babe lying in a
manger. The shepherds told Mary and Joseph what they had seen, what
the angel had announced. And when they left the stable, they told all
who would listen "the good news." All who heard the tale wondered at
what the shepherds had seen and heard. But Mary, thoughtful and
serene in her courage, kept these things to herself and pondered them in
her heart.

Detail of *The Presentation in the Temple* by Rembrandt
About 1660. Mauritshuis, The Hague

nd at the end of eight days, when he was circumcised, he was called Jesus, the name given by the angel before he was conceived in the womb.

And when the time came for their purification according to the law of Moses, they brought him up to Jerusalem to present him to the Lord (as it is written in the law of the Lord, "Every male that opens the womb shall be called holy to the Lord")

and to offer a sacrifice according to what is said in the law of the Lord, "a pair of turtledoves, or two young pigeons."

Now there was a man in Jerusalem, whose name was Simeon, and this man was righteous and devout, looking for the consolation of Israel, and the Holy Spirit was upon him.

And it had been revealed to him by the Holy
Spirit that he should not see death before he
had seen the Lord's Christ.

And inspired by the Spirit he came into the
temple; and when the parents brought in the
child Jesus,

to do for him according to the custom of the
law, he took him up in his arms and blessed
God and said,

"Lord, now lettest thou thy servant
depart in peace,
according to thy word;
for mine eyes have seen thy salvation
which thou hast prepared in the presence of all peoples,
a light for revelation to the Gentiles,
and for glory to thy people Israel."

And his father and his mother marveled at
what was said about him. . .

Luke 2: 21-33

When the Infant was eight days old, He was taken to Jerusalem to the Temple for purification according to the law of Moses. He was, according to God's covenant with Abraham, circumcised. And He was, as instructed by the angel of the Lord, then named Jesus.

Jews in the time of Jesus lived a rich religious life. Every important event in the life of the individual and in the life of the family was accompanied by a rite, religious, and often sacrificial, in character. The center of the religious life of all Jews was the great Temple. At times of high feasts and other important events, Jews journeyed to Jerusalem, to the Temple.

The Temple in the time of Jesus was the third structure that had been constructed on the Rock of Abraham, the site, by tradition, where Abraham had been prepared to sacrifice his son Isaac to the Lord. Jesus was taken to the Temple of Herod, which was begun around 20 B.C. by Herod the Great. This structure, which was the last Jewish structure to be built over the Rock of Abraham, was leveled to the ground by the Romans in A.D. 70.

The first Temple on this site was built by Solomon, son of David, and was destroyed by the invading armies of Nebuchadnezzar. The innermost sanctum of the Temple of Solomon was called the "Holy of Holies" and contained the Ark of the Covenant, the cask that held the tablets upon which God had written His commandments to the chosen people.

The second Temple was hurriedly built at the end of the Babylonian exile and was far less elaborate than the Temple of Solomon. The Ark and the Tablets of the Lord had, of course, been lost. Herod pulled down the second Temple to make way for the third, which was, according to accounts, the most magnificent structure in the world. Even the Romans were awed by its walls of white marble and gold.

A Jewish family with a newborn first son was required to celebrate at least two religious rites shortly after the birth. The mother, considered ritually unclean for forty days after childbirth, was to bring a lamb and a pigeon or dove to the priest in the Temple for sacrifice. A poor woman could omit the lamb and bring two birds. This Mary did.

A second rite celebrated the gift of a first-born male to the family and required the sacrifice of a beast, either a bull or a ram, as a sign of the child's redemption. The second rite, perhaps combined with the first, Mary and Joseph had performed for Jesus. It is likely that pigeons or doves were substituted for the sacrificial beast.

Jesus' presentation to the Lord was, however, exceptional. A man named Simeon recognized, in the Infant, the Messiah. The man, about whom we know nothing, took the eight-day-old Jesus from Mary, and holding the Baby in his arms, he prayed aloud:

> "Lord, now lettest thou thy servant
> depart in peace,
> according to thy word;
> for mine eyes have seen thy salvation. . ."

Simeon, however, saw more in Jesus, more than even Mary and Joseph understood. Jesus was more than the Jews' Messiah. He was the Christ, the Savior of all mankind:

> ". . .a light for revelation to the Gentiles,
> and for glory to thy people Israel."

Detail of *Adoration of the Magi* by Rembrandt
About 1650. Göteborg Museum, Göteborg, Sweden

ow when Jesus was born in Bethlehem of Judea in the days of Herod the king, behold, wise men from the East came to Jerusalem, saying, "Where is he who has been born king of the Jews? For we have seen his star in the East, and have come to worship him."

When Herod the king heard this, he was troubled, and all Jerusalem with him; and assembling all the chief priests and scribes of the people, he inquired of them where the Christ was to be born.

They told him, "In Bethlehem of Judea; for so it is written by the prophet:

'And you, O Bethlehem, in the land of Judah, are by no means least among the rulers of Judah; for from you shall come a ruler who will govern my people Israel.'"

Then Herod summoned the wise men secretly and ascertained from them what time the star appeared;

and he sent them to Bethlehem, saying, "Go
and search diligently for the child,
and when you have found him bring me word,
that I too may come and worship him."
When they had heard the king they went their
way; and lo, the star which they had seen in
the East went before them, till it came to rest
over the place where the child was.
When they saw the star, they rejoiced
exceedingly with great joy;
and going into the house they saw the child
with Mary his mother, and they fell down and
worshiped him. Then, opening their treasures,
they offered him gifts, gold and frankincense
and myrrh.
And being warned in a dream not to return to
Herod, they departed to their own country by
another way.

Matthew 2: 1-12

On the night Jesus was born, a star appeared in the sky. Wise men in the east, perhaps Arabian or Babylonian astrologers, men who spent their days studying the stars, resolved that the appearance of this star was an omen—a sign that a king of the Jews had been born. So they set off for Judea. They traveled to Jerusalem, and because they were respected men of learning, they were received in the court of Herod, king of Judea. Assuming that Herod would know of an event of such significance, they asked: "Where is he, the newborn king of the Jews? We have come to worship him."

Matthew writes that Herod was troubled, as was all of Jerusalem, that is, all of the powerful men who surrounded the king. Herod was rightly troubled by the news of a birth of a king of the Jews; he was not the rightful king of Judea. Herod had been placed upon the throne of David by the Romans, but he was not, by birth, a Jew. He practiced the Jewish religion, and he built the great Temple as a show of piety. But this fooled no one. The righteous Jews of Israel despised Herod. They despised his wanton behavior, his ten wives, his cruelty, and his relentless lust for power. And he was obsessed with power, with retaining what power he had, as well as gathering to himself whatever more he could amass. So upon the instruction of priests who knew of the prophecies, Herod sent the wise men to Bethlehem, saying: "When you find him, bring me word, so I may come and worship as well." When you find the threat to my power, bring me word, so I may come and destroy that threat.

Under the guidance of the star, which reappeared, the wise men found the Child with Mary, His mother. They bowed before Him and worshiped Him. They offered up their treasures: gold, the gift of substance, of livelihood, that He would not want in life; frankincense, a rare fragrance, that He would know the inner treasure of thought; and finally myrrh, a very rare and precious herb used by the Egyptians for embalming, that He, through this bitter substance, that is, through disappointment, would know the joy of total agreement with God. And, knowing of Herod's plots, the wise men departed for their own country without revealing the Child's whereabouts.

The story of the wise men is mysterious. It is filled with omens; with strange men bearing wondrous and exotic gifts; with tyrannical men who will stop at nothing to gain their own ends. But what does it imply? Of what significance is this to us?

When Jesus was presented to the Lord, a man, Simeon, who was also mysterious, who also appeared from out of nowhere, recognized, in the Child, the long-awaited Messiah of the Jews. But he perceived something beyond:

> . . .mine eyes have seen thy salvation
> which thou hast prepared in the presence of all peoples,
> a light for revelation to the Gentiles,
> and for glory to thy people Israel.

Simeon saw that Jesus, the embodiment of God's salvation, was sent for *all* peoples. He was a revelation to the gentiles, as well as a glory to the people of Israel.

The magi, the wise men of the east, were gentiles. They knew nothing of the prophecies of Isaiah, Jeremiah, and Micah. They did not come simply to pay homage to a new king of the Jews. As Simeon foretold in the Temple, they too saw, in a star, in a light, the revelation of God's salvation.

Detail of *Flight into Egypt* by Duccio
About 1300. Opera del Duoma, Sienna, Italy

ow when they had de-
parted, behold, an angel of
the Lord appeared to Joseph in a dream and
said, "Rise, take the child and his mother, and
flee to Egypt, and remain there till I tell you;
for Herod is about to search for the child, to
destroy him."
And he rose and took the child and his mother
by night, and departed to Egypt, and remained
there until the death of Herod.
This was to fulfil what the Lord had spoken by
the prophet, "Out of Egypt have I called my
son."

Matthew 2: 13-15

ow, when the wise men had departed Bethlehem, an angel of the Lord appeared to Joseph in a dream. And the angel told Joseph that Herod was searching for the newborn Messiah. If the king's soldiers found the Baby, He would be murdered. Joseph must take the Baby and His mother out of Judea, beyond the long reach of Herod.

Herod had learned, through the priests in the Temple, of the prophecies that a Branch of David, that is, a legitimate heir to the throne of Judea, would be born in Bethlehem. The king had also learned, through the appearance of foreign wise men, who understood such omens as the appearance of a new star, that such a child had, in fact, been born. When the wise men did not return with the information Herod sought, he ordered that a search for the Child be started.

Herod the Great walked a political tightrope throughout his reign. He had been appointed King of Judea by the Roman Senate, which had rubber-stamped the appointment to please Caesar Augustus. Herod's power was based entirely in Rome. His job was to keep the economy of Judea running smoothly and to send the wealth, provided by that economy, out of Judea and into the coffers of the Roman Empire. To accomplish this, Herod had to keep the people of Judea, the Jews, contented. Unrest at home upset that flow of wealth, which upset Rome, which upset Caesar, who was the source of all power. Herod, a skillful politician, was well aware that his entire existence depended upon keeping the machinery well oiled and functioning. This he managed to do for more than forty years. It was not, however, an easy job.

The Jews loathed Herod. They loathed him when he was appointed king, and they loathed him when he died. He was, to begin with, an Edomite, and the Edomites were ancient enemies of the Jews. The Edomites had refused the children of Israel, on their way to the

The Sinai, *through which Joseph and Mary and the Baby Jesus journeyed in their flight to Egypt, is a bleak landscape of mountainous desert dotted with oases. Some Biblical scholars believe that the Holy Family remained near some oasis in the Sinai during those years away from Judea. The Peninsula was then, as it is now, a part of Egypt.*

Rest on the Flight to Egypt
by Caravaggio
About 1615.
Doria Pamphily Gallery, Rome

promised land, passage across Edom. Moses declared them archenemies,
and they remained such through the centuries that followed.

Herod, throughout his reign, tried to please the Jews. He
converted to their religion, and he took as his bride a Hasmonean
princess, that is, a member of the Hebrew family that had ruled Judea
before Herod. He also rebuilt the Temple, loading it with greater
splendor than even Solomon could have imagined. None of this,
however, convinced the Jews that Herod was anything but an Edomite
usurper. At every turn, they plotted against him.

Mariamne, Herod's Hasmonean wife, plotted against him, as did
her family, who felt that one of their own should rightfully sit on the
throne. The plots went on and on, and Herod's palace in Jerusalem
became mired in endless intrigue. Herod had Mariamne's uncle, who
was high priest of the Temple, murdered. He had Mariamne's great
uncle, another priest, executed. Then, Mariamne was tried, found
guilty, and put to death. Mariamne's mother was next. But still the
plots, both real and imagined, continued. In the end, Herod put his
own sons, his sons by Mariamne, to death.

By the time of the birth of Jesus, Herod the Great had descended
into a relentless nightmare of paranoia. If a rightful heir to the throne of
David had been born, then he must be found, found and destroyed. If
anyone around whom the Jews would rally appeared, then he must be
destroyed.

Joseph, fully aware that a man who murders his own sons will stop
at nothing, saw that the only wise course was to flee beyond the reach
of Herod. So Joseph took the Child and the Child's mother and
departed Judea for Egypt. And they stayed there, in Egypt, until Joseph
heard that Herod was dead and in his grave.

Detail of *Massacre of the Innocents* by Guido Reni
1611. Pinacoteca, Bologna, Italy

Then Herod, when he saw that he had been tricked by the wise men, was in a furious rage, and he sent and killed all the male children in Bethlehem and in all that region who were two years old or under, according to the time which he had ascertained from the wise men. Then was fulfilled what was spoken by the prophet Jeremiah:

"A voice was heard in Ramah,
wailing and loud lamentation,
Rachel weeping for her children;
she refused to be consoled,
because they were no more."

But when Herod died, behold, an angel of the Lord appeared in a dream to Joseph in Egypt, saying,
"Rise, take the child and his mother, and go to the land of Israel, for those who sought the child's life are dead."

And he rose and took the child and his
mother, and went to the land of Israel.
But when he heard that Archelaus reigned
over Judea in place of his father Herod, he was
afraid to go there, and being warned in a
dream he withdrew to the district of Galilee.
And he went and dwelt in a city called
Nazareth, that what was spoken by the
prophets might be fulfilled, "He shall be called
a Nazarene."

Matthew 2: 16-23

When Herod realized that he had been tricked by the wise men of the east, his rage knew no limits. He sent soldiers into Bethlehem with orders that all male children two years old and younger should be put to the sword. And this was done in Bethlehem and in all the region around Bethlehem. And the parents of the slaughtered children mourned their loss as the prophet Jeremiah had foretold:

Thus says the Lord:
"A voice is heard in Ramah,
     lamentation and bitter weeping.
Rachel·is weeping for her children;
     she refuses to be comforted for her
          children,
     because they are not."

Jeremiah 31: 15

Cries of anguish were raised on the earth. Mothers wept for their children. They wept and refused to be consoled because they could find no meaning, no understanding of why life on earth is filled with such pain.

Mary and Joseph had escaped, saving the Baby Jesus from the slaughter. They had gone down into Egypt, where they lived until Joseph, in a dream, learned that Herod was dead. It was then safe to return to Israel. But when they returned to the land of Israel, Joseph discovered that Herod's wicked son, Archelaus, reigned over Judea. And in another dream, Joseph was warned not to return to Bethlehem, the city of David, the city of his family. So Mary and Joseph and Jesus moved, then, on to Galilee, which was ruled over by another son of Herod, Herod Antipas, who was less ruthless than his brother. They went and lived in the town of Nazareth. And by this change of plan, what had been foretold by the prophets was fulfilled:

"He shall be called a Nazarene."

The **Wailing Wall** in Jerusalem (above) is the last remnant of the Temple of Herod the Great, where Jesus was presented to the Lord and where He worshiped. The western, or Wailing, wall was part of a system of retaining walls that completely surrounded Mount Moriah, creating the Temple Mount, a platform more than one million square feet in area. The Temple (reconstructed model, left) was then built directly over the Rock of Abraham. With walls of white marble and gold, it was described as "appearing in the sunlight like a snow-covered mountain." In A.D. 70, Roman legions, after more than three years of fighting, crushed a Jewish revolt, led by the Zealots, and leveled the great Temple. Scenes of the destruction and plunder can still be seen carved on the Arch of Titus in the Forum in Rome.

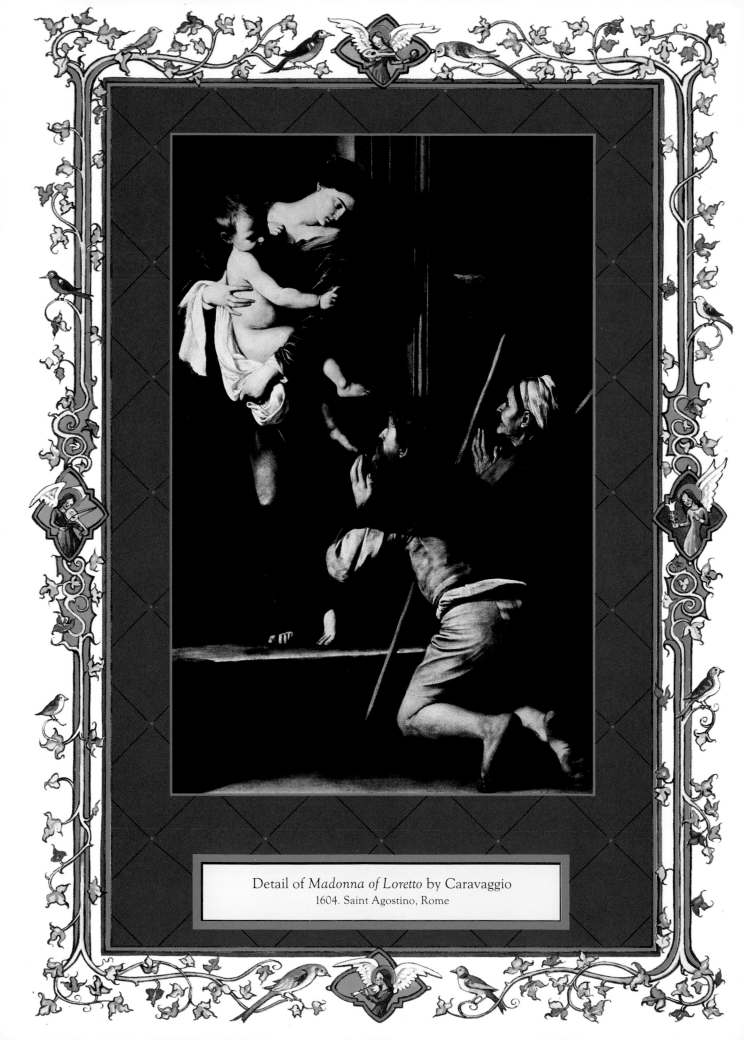

Detail of *Madonna of Loretto* by Caravaggio
1604. Saint Agostino, Rome

And the child grew and became strong, filled with wisdom; and the favor of God was upon him.

Luke 2: 40

Christmas in Bethlehem. The words evoke images of a silent, reverent, alabaster city, waiting expectantly on a quiet and starry night. The realities of Christmas in modern-day Bethlehem are, however, very different. The endless conflict in the Middle East guarantees the presence of troops whenever and wherever crowds gather for major festivals. And the tendency of modern societies to make commercial capital on any event or place of importance is not absent in Bethlehem. The town's aggressive merchants loudly hawk their wares—even on Christmas Eve and Day. Nor can the jostling, noisy—sometimes raucous—character of life in Middle Eastern cultures be ignored.

Perhaps, most importantly, the Christians who come to Bethlehem to celebrate Christmas are no longer a unified group. Today, Eastern Christians—including Greek and Syrian Orthodox, Egyptian Coptics, and many others—and Western Christians—including Roman Catholics, Anglicans, Lutherans, and many other Protestant groups—all have a claim on Bethlehem's Christmas. In fact, not all Christians celebrate Jesus' nativity on the same date. In the West, Christians celebrate Christmas on December 25, a date established in Rome at the time of the empire. Eastern Christians, however, continue to celebrate the Nativity on or after January 6—Epiphany in the West—depending upon the calendar used.

As a result of Christianity's fragmentation, many shrines are held exclusively by one body; others are debated as to authenticity; and different groups maintain competing shrines. Many of the most important Christian holy places are in the hands of the Eastern Orthodox. This is the Christian church that received its legacy from the ancient church of the Eastern Roman Empire and then, later, from the successor state of the Byzantine Empire. Despite the fall of Constantinople and, with it, the Christian Empire of Byzantine Rome in A.D. 1453, the Eastern Orthodox Church has, down through the centuries, held on to many of its holy places. And so it is that the holiest place in Bethlehem, the Church of the Nativity—traditional site of the birth of Jesus—is held by the Eastern Orthodox. To a lesser extent, the Roman Catholics, known as "Latin Christians" in the Middle East, hold important Christian sites in the Holy Land. These are largely the legacy of the Crusades of the Middle Ages, when Crusader armies of France, Germany, and other western Catholic lands conquered the Holy Land for pope and church.

Yet division is not the whole story of Christmas in the Holy Land. Churches share their holy places, and Christians generally treat each other with respect, each group of worshipers celebrating according to their individual customs and rites. The Eastern Orthodox, for example, share with other Christian groups special worship privileges in certain parts of the Church of the Nativity.

The residents of Bethlehem and nearby areas watch the celebrations come and go, some participating, some selling wares in streetside bazaars, some merely observing. On December 24, Bethlehem witnesses Christmas Eve celebrations of Protestant and Roman Catholic Christians.

For Roman Catholics, Christmas in the Holy Land begins with the Christmas Eve procession to Bethlehem by the Latin Patriarch of Jerusalem—highest Roman Catholic Church authority in the Holy Land. The distance is only about five miles. This is the same route that many pilgrims and tourists visiting the Holy Land during Christmas follow. The road leaves Jerusalem and winds its way through the hilly terrain. At this time of year, the rainy season is normally in progress, and the hills take on a fresh, springlike, greenish hue. Limestone outcroppings punctuate the roadside, and occasional flocks of sheep dot the hillsides. Ancient cypress trees and olive groves laden with grayish-green fruit, their trunks gnarled and woody, shade, in places, the road to Bethlehem.

On the approach to Bethlehem, the procession passes Rachel's tomb, a small, white, domed structure—revered as a shrine by Judaism. As the Patriarch's motorcade nears the town, growing crowds line the street. The procession now moves through narrow streets flanked by tall stone houses. Bells ring, and children, crying out joyously, run after the Patriarch's automobile.

The narrow street suddenly opens into a square. Packed with people, reverberating with the noisy sounds of the crowd and the pealing of bells, Manger Square teems on this afternoon with the vitality of a festival and the noise and smells of a Middle Eastern bazaar. Arab craftspeople sell religious items they have made—crèche scenes and crucifixes made of native olivewood inlaid with mother-of-pearl mosaics. Others sell foods—shish kebab, pita bread, lamb or mutton—to hungry tourists who await the celebrations.

The Roman Catholic Patriarch of Jerusalem annually leads a procession of pilgrims to Bethlehem on Christmas Eve.

Christmas Eve crowds fill Manger Square, a large public space opposite the Church of the Nativity in Bethlehem.

Christmas Eve celebrations in Manger Square include children's choirs singing carols.

The destination of the Catholic pilgrims is not, however, this boisterous square, but rather, the plaza at the eastern end of the square, around which clusters a medieval-looking complex of buildings. In the center of these buildings stands the Church of the Nativity, the holiest place in Bethlehem, built over the site of Jesus' birth. The church itself is an Orthodox shrine, but three Christian churches, the Orthodox, the Roman Catholics, and the Armenians, share rights to the Grotto of the Manger underneath—traditional site of Jesus' birth.

Oldest of churches in the Holy Land, the exterior of the Church of the Nativity looks more like a fortress than a church. It is, in fact, something of a medieval fortress, fortified by occupying Crusader forces in the Middle Ages as a bulwark against Arab invaders. Great, stone walls surround the entire compound.

The history of the Church of the Nativity goes back far beyond the times of the Crusaders. It was founded in about A.D. 325 by the first Christian Roman emperor—Constantine. The emperor's mother, Helena, on an earlier pilgrimage to the Holy Land, identified this spot as the site of Jesus' birth. Severely damaged in a rebellion centuries later, the church was, in the A.D. 500's, rebuilt magnificently by the great Byzantine Emperor Justinian. The basic design of today's church remains approximately the same as Justinian's, although, of course, many changes have been made over the last fourteen centuries.

Within the fortified walls of the Church of the Nativity compound, churches and buildings of other faiths—St. Catherine's Roman Catholic Church, an Armenian monastery—nestle together. Also within the walls are courtyards, gardens, and, underground, limestone caves.

The chief Roman Catholic service of the Nativity begins late in the evening on Christmas Eve at St. Catherine's, where a great crowd gathers. The bells ring out joyfully before the service, a solemn High Mass, begins. The Patriarch of Jerusalem leads the service at the high altar, accompanied by other clergy and acolytes. Splendid vestments, clouds of incense, and the strains of choirs contribute to a sense of holiness. At the same time, crowds jostle and make noise, more in joyous celebration than irreverence.

The height of the celebration, which occurs after midnight, is the procession from St. Catherine's to the Grotto of the Manger underneath the Church of the Nativity. Led by the Patriarch, the solemn procession files out of the Roman Catholic church, winds across the flagstones of the courtyard, and enters the great and ancient Church of the Nativity. Here the procession follows a carefully prescribed path, a reminder that adherents of many faiths hold Christian observances in this place. The walls of the church—dark, massive, largely unadorned—bear testimony to its ancientness. Here and there, a remnant of a fresco or mosaic, the work of Byzantine or Crusader craftworkers, shines in the light cast from innumerable candles and oil lamps. Colonnades lead the eye down the church's nave toward the front, to the icon screen that walls off the Greek Orthodox high altar. The procession then turns and descends stone steps that are hollowed by the feet of innumerable pilgrims who have, for the last fourteen hundred years, followed this path down into the Grotto where, by tradition, Christ was born.

A Roman Catholic Mass is held before the high altar at the Church of the Holy Sepulchre.

Worshipers follow clergy, crowding into the Grotto, neither wider nor longer than a railroad car. The cramped, packed space is luminous with candles and heady with incense; stone walls echo with chanting. At the spot claimed by tradition to be the place of Jesus' birth, an inlaid fourteen-point silver star gleams in the floor. It is here that the most holy rite of this Christmas Eve service is enacted. The Patriarch reverently takes an effigy of the Christ Child and ritually lays it on the place of birth. Shortly afterward, the procession forms again and retraces its steps back to the Church of St. Catherine, where services conclude.

On this same night, other Christians celebrate the birth of Jesus in different ways. One celebration takes place not in the town of Bethlehem, but out in a field on its eastern fringe. Maintained by the Y.M.C.A., this "shepherd's field" draws several thousand pilgrims, mostly Protestant Christians, to the spot where, by tradition, the shepherds heard the angels' Christmas message. This is one of the contested holy places: the Eastern Orthodox and Roman Catholic churches have rival "shepherd's fields" near Bethlehem. No one claim can establish absolute credibility. (The location is, nonetheless, generally believed to be east of Bethlehem.)

But these claims and counterclaims do not concern the pilgrims who have gathered for a Christmas Eve celebration of Christmas carols. And the field itself, in a rural, pastoral area away from the town's lights and noise, seems authentic. A large, walled-in enclosure accommodates

An archbishop of the Eastern Orthodox Church presides over a Christmas service in the Church of the Nativity.

A Roman Catholic Mass is celebrated on Christmas Eve at St. Catherine's in Bethlehem.

the Christmas pilgrims. A choir leads the crowd, composed of Westerners and a few Arab Christians, in such familiar carols as "The First Noël," "O Come, All Ye Faithful," "Hark, the Herald Angels Sing," and "Silent Night." In the crisp night air under the starlit skies, with the sound of voices united in song, one can easily imagine shepherds in these fields twenty centuries ago, the nocturnal silence of their watch broken by the multitude of the heavenly host. Though quite unlike the rich liturgies celebrated in Bethlehem's great churches, the simple outdoor celebration is a moving and unforgettable experience for its participants.

The sounds of still other Christmas celebrations—those of Greek and Syrian Orthodox Christians, Armenian Christians, and others—will ring out in Bethlehem and the surrounding regions in the coming weeks. From mid-December through mid-January, Bethlehem looks on as Christians of almost every ethnic identity and confession of faith come to its doorstep to celebrate. Though different in many particulars, all are united by the Christmas story itself and by the hope it brings to the world through every age and in all places.

Crafts

Pretzel Nativity Scene

Materials
- packaged pretzel sticks (rods and mini-twist)
- pipe cleaners
- colored construction paper
- paper doilies (6-in.; 10-in.)
- cotton balls
- aluminum foil
- 0000 fine steel wool
- adhesive tape, 1/2-in. wide
- fine-tipped markers or acrylic craft paint
- small paintbrush and water (if using paint)
- salt dough (see recipe, page 67)
- scissors*
- serrated knife†
- toothpicks
- cookie sheet
- white glue
- ruler
- glue gun (optional)†
- clear craft spray (optional)†

---

*If children are involved, use snubbed-nose scissors.
†This part of the craft *should not* be attempted without adult supervision.

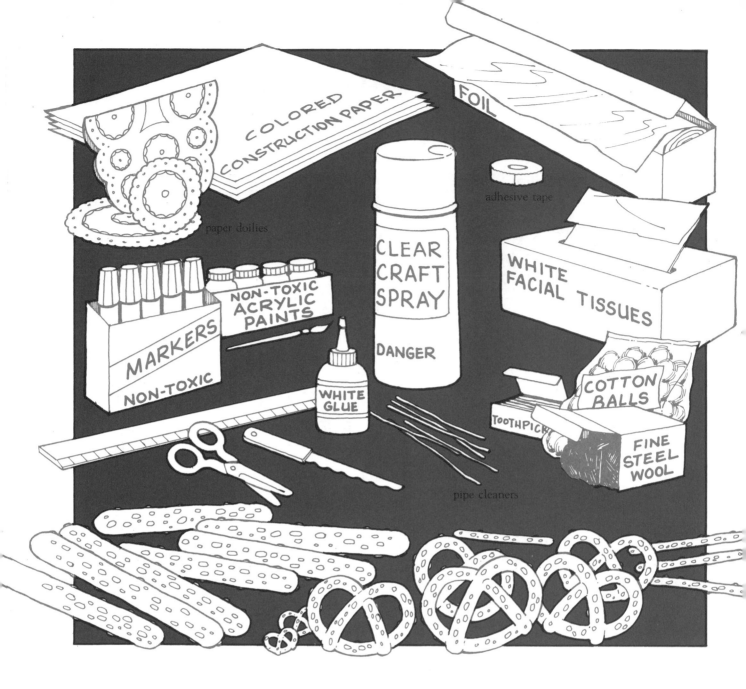

Working with Pretzels

For some of the nativity figures, you will need to cut the pretzels into various lengths. This works best if you use a serrated knife to gently saw the pretzel at the desired length. Children working on this portion of the project should be carefully supervised.

Pretzels glue together easily with white glue, but will take some time for each joint to dry. A quicker method is to use a glue gun, but such a tool should be operated only by an adult.

If you plan to save your nativity figures, seal the pretzels with a coat of clear craft spray. Spray the figures after the glued joints have dried, but before other materials, such as paper or cotton, have been added. And always spray in a well-ventilated area, away from children.

Read through the directions before you begin to work. Then assign each family member a job that fits his or her abilities. It will probably take several hours to complete all of the figures, so you may wish to plan two or three work sessions. Organize your supplies so that they can be put away and reassembled easily.

Figures with Salt Dough Heads and Hands

Make the salt dough using the recipe at the right. Since molded salt dough takes several hours to dry, it is best to make all the salt dough parts at one time. These include all heads and hands and the wise men's gifts. For suggestions for shaping the gifts, see the illustrations accompanying the instructions for individual wise men. Paint and decorate these pieces any way you wish.

Salt dough will air-dry overnight if the parts are not too thick. The process can be quickened by using the oven. Preheat the oven to 300° F. (149°C). Place the salt dough figures on a cookie sheet lined with waxed paper. After the oven reaches the designated temperature, turn it off and immediately place the salt dough figures in the oven. The dough should dry in about two hours. One word of caution: The faster salt dough dries, the greater the chance it will develop surface cracks. If this should happen, simply fill in the cracks with additional salt dough.

Once dried, the dough figures may be colored with markers or painted with acrylic craft paint. Again, a coat of acrylic craft spray will help preserve your figures from year to year. However, glue the heads onto the pretzel rods and allow the joints to dry before spraying.

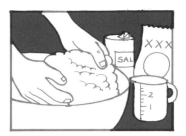

Salt Dough Recipe

1 cup flour   1/2 cup water
1/2 cup salt

Mix flour and salt. Add water. Mix well. If dough is sticky, gradually work in small amounts of flour with your hands until the dough is easy to work with. Use immediately.

Instructions for heads

1. Crush aluminum foil into a 1½-inch ball, about the size of a ping-pong ball.
2. Cover the ball with a thin layer of salt dough.
3. Form a face, using a toothpick for outlining and small bits of salt dough for features such as a nose and beard. Other facial details and color can be painted on after the heads are dry.

Instructions for hands

1. Form a ½-inch ball of salt dough.
2. Flatten the ball slightly.
3. Use scissors to cut a slit to form a thumb. (Note: Make hands in pairs.)
4. Use a toothpick to outline the fingers.
5. With a toothpick, form a hole in the bottom of each hand, at the point where the hand attaches to the arm. (Later, a pipe cleaner will be glued into this hole.)
6. Bend the fingers down on one of the hands to allow a shepherd to hold a staff.

Begin all human figures using these basic steps:

1. From construction paper, cut a circle 7½ inches, a square 3 inches, and a rectangle 4 inches by 5 inches. (For color suggestions, see the instructions for each figure.)

2. Fold the circle in half and cut along the fold.

3. Tape the edges of one half-circle together to form a cone.

4. Cut off the point of the cone to allow the pretzel to slide in. Glue in place.

5. Cut a pretzel rod 5½ inches long.

6. Place the head on the cut end of the pretzel. Twist the head gently to round out the end of the pretzel. Brush off loose crumbs. Glue the head onto the pretzel. Allow to dry.

7. Tightly wrap the square around the pretzel rod just below the head. Glue in place.

8. Fold the rectangle in half lengthwise. Glue a pipe cleaner along the inside fold and glue the rectangle closed.

9. Placing the thumbs up, glue a hand on each end of the pipe cleaner.

Mary

Follow steps 1-9 on page 68 with these variations:

1. Cut a pretzel rod 4½ in hes long.

2. Use blue paper for the circle, square, and rectangle.

3. Cut a triangle from the bottom edge of the sleeves. Glue the center of the sleeves onto Mary's back.

4. Glue 0000 fine steel wool to Mary's head for hair.

5. For a scarf, cut a 7¾-inch blue circle in half. Accordion fold one half; glue to head.

6. From a doily, cut a halo and decorations; glue in place.

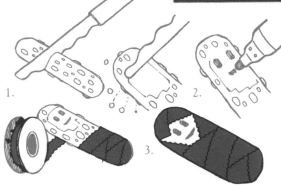

Jesus

1. Cut a pretzel rod 2½ inches long.

2. Gently scrape off the brown coating at one end of the pretzel for the head. Draw a face with marker.

3. Wrap the pretzel with adhesive tape, leaving only the face showing.

Joseph

Follow steps 1-9 on page 68 with these variations:

1. Use dark brown paper for the circle, square, and rectangle.

2. Prepare the sleeves as in step 3 for Mary.

3. From black paper, cut a narrow strip 6 inches long for a belt. Fringe the ends. Glue it around Joseph's waist.

4. Cut a rectangle 8 inches by 4 inches from yellow paper for Joseph's cloak. With markers, draw colored stripes the length of the rectangle.

5. Fold the rectangle in half. Cut a triangle-shaped notch at the center of the fold to form a neck hole. Open the rectangle and cut a slit from the narrow end to the neck hole as shown.

6. Put the cloak over Joseph's shoulders and cross the front halves. Glue in place.

7. Drape a facial tissue over the head. Draw colored stripes on a pipe cleaner. Wrap the pipe cleaner around the head to hold the tissue in place. Twist the ends. Glue if necessary.

First Wise Man

Follow steps 1-9 on page 68 with these variations:

1. Use purple paper for the circle, square, and rectangle.

2. Prepare the sleeves as in step 3 for Mary.

3. Make a belt as in step 3 for Joseph, but with pointed ends.

4. For a vest, cut a rectangle of pink paper 2½ inches by 6 inches.

5. Fold the rectangle in half and cut a notch at the center of the fold to form a neck hole.

6. Cut the bottom edge of the vest into a point as shown.

7. Decorate the vest and sleeves with markers. Slit the vest from one point to the neck hole. Put the vest on and glue at back.

8. For a crown, cut a foil rectangle 3 inches by 5 inches. Fold the foil in thirds to form a strip 1 inch by 5 inches.

9. Cut triangles along one edge of the strip. Wrap it around the head. Cut to fit. Glue in place.

10. Cover a cotton ball with a facial tissue. Trim excess tissue. Glue the ball inside the crown.

Second Wise Man

Follow steps 1-9 on page 68 with these variations:

1. Use red paper for the circle, square, and rectangle.

2. Prepare the sleeves as in step 3 for Mary.

3. Using purple paper, prepare a belt as in step 3 for Joseph.

4. Using orange paper, prepare a cloak as in steps 4 and 5 for Joseph. Make the stripes brown.

5. Put the cloak on and glue.

6. Cover a pipe cleaner with foil. Place it around the wise man's neck as a chain.

7. Drape a facial tissue over the head. Glue in place.

8. Cut a strip of foil 1 inch by 5 inches for a crown. Fold it in half twice. Cut notches along one edge of the strip. Wrap it around the head. Cut to fit. Glue in place.

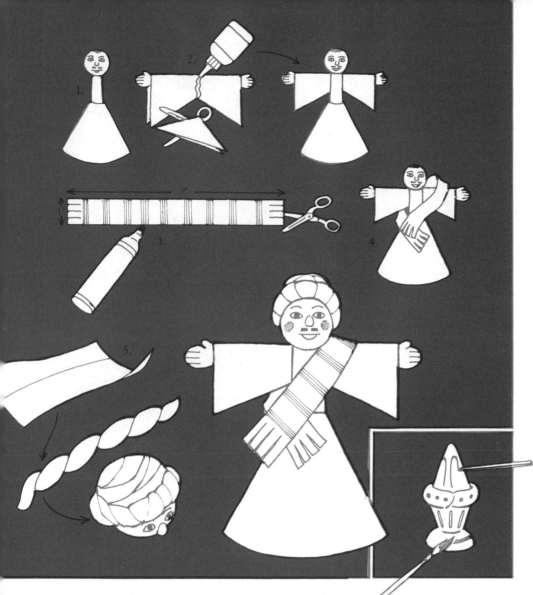

Third Wise Man
Follow steps 1-9 on page 68
with these variations:

Third Wise Man
1. Use dark blue paper for the circle, square, and rectangle.
2. Prepare the sleeves as in step 3 for Mary.
3. Cut a strip of yellow paper 1 inch by 9 inches. Draw colored stripes on it and fringe the ends.
4. Drape the strip over the wise man's shoulder. Cross the ends and glue in place.
5. Tightly twist two facial tissues into rope shapes. Coil and glue them around the head to form a turban.

fold in half

fold again

7.

8.

When the three wise men are completed, bend their arms and glue the salt dough gifts to their hands as shown.

Angel

Follow steps 1-9 on page 68 with these variations:

1. Use white paper for the circle, square, and rectangle.

2. Cut a 6-inch doily in half. Cut out a small half-circle at the center of the straight edge of one of the halves.

3. Glue the cut half of the doily around the cone to make a lacy skirt.

4. Fold a 6-inch doily in half and glue it over the sleeves.

Glue the sleeves to the back of the angel.

5. To make hair, gently pull apart a cotton ball. Glue it to the angel's head.

6. Fold a 10-inch doily in half. Cut out the center as shown. Glue the centerpiece to the angel's head for a halo.

7. Cut a 6-inch doily in half. Glue the two halves inside the bottom edge of the folded 10-inch doily as shown.

8. Glue this entire wing piece onto the back of the angel.

Shepherd

Follow steps 1-9 on page 68 with these variations:

1. Use dark green paper for the circle, square, and rectangle. Draw black and red stripes before cutting out the shapes.

2. Prepare the sleeves as in step 3 for Mary.

3. For a cloak, cut a 6-inch circle of white paper. Cut the circle in half. Fold one half-circle in half and cut out the shape shown in the diagram.

4. Draw marks on the cloak to give the appearance of wool fleece. Place the cloak over the left shoulder and glue it in place.

5. Color a pipe cleaner brown and bend it into a staff. Glue it to the shepherd's curled fingers.

6. Glue on 0000 fine steel wool for hair.

7. Drape a facial tissue over the head. Draw colored stripes on a pipe cleaner. Wrap the pipe cleaner around the head to hold the tissue in place. Twist the ends. Glue if necessary.

73

Camel

1. Using pretzel rods, cut camel parts to the lengths shown in the diagram. Cut the neck, head, and body at 45° angles.

2. Glue the neck, head, and body together.

3. Gently rub the cut end of each leg along the camel's back to round out the joint for a proper fit.

4. Glue the legs to the body.

5. Cut a circle 7¾ inches in diameter of brown construction paper.

6. Fold and cut the circle in half.

7. Tape the edges of one half-circle together to make a cone.

8. Flatten the cone. Fold the point down 1 inch and tape in place.

9. Cut off a bottom corner of the flattened cone.

10. Glue the cone over the camel's back with the cut corner toward the neck.

11. Repeat steps 6-10 using a 6-inch doily.

12. To make a tail, fringe a small strip of brown paper and glue it to the end of a thin pretzel stick. Glue the tail under the back of the folded cone.

13. For reins, twist a pipe cleaner around the camel's nose. Twist two pipe cleaners together and bend them over the neck. Fasten the pipe cleaners together as shown. Bend half of a pipe cleaner over the camel's head and glue in place.

14. With black marker, draw a face. Decorate the doily and pipe cleaners with colored markers.

15. Glue brown paper ears to the head behind the reins.

Cow

1. Using pretzel rods, cut cow parts to the lengths shown in the diagram. Cut the head and neck at 45° angles.

2. Glue the four body pretzels together. Glue the head to the neck.

3. Use a mini-twist pretzel for the udder. Cut ⅛-inch pieces from the ends of three pretzel sticks. Glue four ends to the udder for teats. Glue two ends to the head for horns. Glue the udder under the body.

4. Glue the neck to the body.

5. Rub the cut end of each leg along a pretzel rod to round out the joint for a proper fit. Glue the legs in place.

6. Glue on brown paper ears next to the horns.

7. Draw a face with marker.

8. For a tail, fringe a small piece of brown paper and glue it to one end of a pretzel stick. Cut the other end at a 45° angle and glue the tail in place.

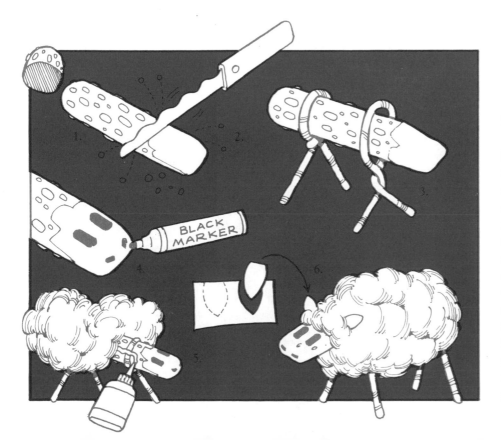

Lamb

1. Cut a pretzel rod 2½ inches long.

2. Gently scrape off the brown coating at the uncut end for the head.

3. Twist two pipe cleaners around the pretzel and spread the ends apart to form legs as shown.

4. Draw a face with black marker.

5. Glue on cotton for the lamb's wool, covering all but the face.

6. Glue on brown or black paper ears.

Recipes

Legends behind the Christmas recipes

The recipes described can be found on this page or on the recipe cards that accompany *Christmas in the Holy Land*.

HOLIDAY WREATH
When King Herod learned from the Wise Men that a King of the Jews had been born, he sent soldiers to find the Infant and kill Him. An ancient Christmas legend tells that Mary hid the Baby Jesus under a holly bush. The holly bush put forth leaves and grew slender thorns to protect the Child from the king's henchmen. When He was safe, the Christ Child then blessed the holly bush so that it would be forever green—a symbol of immortality.

TWELFTH-NIGHT CAKE
Our Christmas cake is made from yeast, which according to legend is a gift of the Christ Child. The Holy Family, trying to escape from Herod's soldiers, knocked on the door of a woman who was kneading bread. The woman wrapped the Child in her dough. When the soldiers burst into her house and searched for the Child, they were unable to find Him. After they left, the woman gave the Child back to His mother. Suddenly the dough began to rise, and there was no end to the amount of bread the woman could bake from it.

CANDY CANE COOKIES
The shape of the candy cane is a symbol of the crook used by shepherds visiting the stable on the night of Jesus' birth. The peppermint fragrance is emblematic of hyssop, an herb used in early purification rites. The colors of the candy cane remind us of both the purity of Jesus and the blood of His sacrifice.

MINCEMEAT PIE
The combination of spices found in mincemeat symbolize the offerings brought to the Baby Jesus by the Wise Men. For centuries, holiday mincemeat pies were made in an oblong shape to represent the manger.

CHRISTMAS STARS
The star—a universal symbol of hope and expectation—appeared on the night of Jesus' birth and led the Wise Men of the East to the Christ Child. Cookies and pastries molded into the shape of a star have for centuries represented the Star of the East.

CANDLEBRAID BREAD
Christmas candles symbolize the journey Mary and Joseph made to Bethlehem and their search for a place to stay that night. Today a candle burning in the window on Christmas Eve tells visitors that this is a house where they are welcome. A candle placed in the center of braided bread is, thus, a symbol of holiday hospitality.

MORAVIAN CHRISTMAS COOKIES
The Pennsylvania Dutch traditionally make Moravian Christmas cookies—both white and brown—in the shape of rabbits, horses, birds, camels, lambs, and other animals. It is their custom to honor animals that are important to their own lives as well as to honor the animals present at the birth of Christ.

MORAVIAN CHRISTMAS COOKIES

Light cookies

1 cup butter or margarine	2 tbsp. heavy cream
2 cups sugar	4 cups all-purpose flour
4 eggs, beaten	

Cream the butter and sugar until the mixture is light and fluffy. Add beaten eggs and cream. Stir in flour. Wrap the dough in plastic and refrigerate either 3 or 4 hours or overnight. Roll out the dough on a lightly floured board to a thickness of 1/8 of an inch. Using cookie cutters, cut out cookies. Place on lightly greased baking sheet. Bake in a preheated oven at 350° F. for 10 to 12 minutes or until the cookies are crisp and a very light golden brown.

Dark cookies

3 3/4 cups flour	1/3 cup brown sugar, firmly packed	1/2 tsp. allspice
3/4 tsp. baking soda	3/4 tsp. ginger	1/2 tsp. nutmeg
1 cup molasses	3/4 tsp. cloves	pinch of salt
1/2 cup butter	3/4 tsp. cinnamon	

Sift the flour. Then sift in the baking soda, salt, and all of the spices. Heat the molasses and butter until the butter melts. Stir in the sugar until it dissolves. Gradually add the flour. Beat after each addition of flour until the dough is smooth. Cover the dough with waxed paper and store in the refrigerator for a week. Roll out the dough thinly, a small amount at a time. Cut with cookie cutters and, if desired, decorate. Bake in a preheated oven at 350° F. for 8 to 10 minutes.

Carols

As With Gladness Men of Old

William C. Dix, 1860

Arranged from Conrad Kocher, 1838

1. As with glad-ness men of old Did the guid-ing star be-hold;
2. As with joy-ful steps they sped To that low-ly man-ger bed,
3. As they of-fered gifts most rare, At that man-ger rude and bare,

As with joy they hailed its light, Lead-ing on-ward, beam-ing bright;
There to bend the knee be-fore Him whom heaven and earth a-dore;
So may we with ho-ly joy, Pure and free from sin's al-loy,

So, most gra-cious Lord, may we Ev-er-more be led to Thee.
So may we with will-ing feet Ev-er seek Thy mer-cy seat.
All our cost-liest treas-ures bring, Christ, to Thee, our heav'n-ly King.

O Little Town of Bethlehem

Phillips Brooks, 1868–1893   Lewis H. Redner, 1868–1908 [WE]

1. O lit-tle town of Beth-le-hem, How still we see thee lie! A-bove thy deep and dream-less sleep The si-lent stars go by; Yet in thy dark streets shin-eth The ev-er-last-ing Light; The hopes and fears of all the years Are met in thee to-night.

2. For Christ is born of Ma-ry, And gath-ered all a-bove, While mor-tals sleep, the an-gels keep Their watch of won-d'ring love. O morn-ing stars to-geth-er Pro-claim the ho-ly birth, And prais-es sing to God the King, And peace to men on earth!

3. How si-lent-ly, how si-lent-ly The won-drous gift is given! So God im-parts to hu-man hearts The bless-ings of His heaven. No ear may hear His com-ing, But in this world of sin, Where meek souls will re-ceive Him still, The dear Christ en-ters in.

4. O ho-ly Child of Beth-le-hem! De-scend to us, we pray; Cast out our sin and en-ter in, Be born in us to-day. We hear the Christ-mas an-gels The great glad tid-ings tell; O come to us, a-bide with us, Our Lord Im-man-u-el!

What Child Is This?

William Dix, ca 1865

17th Century English Air
Arrangement: John Stainer

1. What Child is this, Who, laid to rest On Mary's lap, is sleeping? Whom
2. Why lies He in such mean es-tate, Where ox and ass are feed-ing? Good
3. So bring Him in-cense, gold, and myrrh, Come peas-ant, King to own Him, The

an-gels greet with an-thems sweet, While shep-herds watch are keep-ing?
Chris-tian, fear: for sin-ners here The si-lent Word is plead-ing.
King of kings, sal-va-tion brings, Let lov-ing hearts en-throne Him.

REFRAIN

This, this is Christ the King; Whom shep-herds guard and an-gels sing:
Nails, spear, shall pierce Him through, The Cross be borne, for me, for you:
Raise, raise the song on high, The Vir-gin sings her lull-a-by:

Haste, haste to bring Him laud,
Hail, hail, the Word made flesh, The Babe, the Son of Ma-ry!
Joy, joy, for Christ is born,

ACKNOWLEDGMENTS

Cover: WORLD BOOK photo by Steven Spicer

2: © Jeff Adamo, The Stock Market

6-7: Detail of *Adoration of the Magi* (mid-1500's), an oil painting on canvas from the workshop of Bassano; Pinacoteca, Sansepolcro, Italy (SCALA/Art Resource)

8: *Isaiah* (1512) detail of fresco from the Sistine Ceiling by Michaelangelo; Vatican City (SCALA/Art Resource)

10: *Tree of Jesse* (about 1220), stained glass window by an unknown artist; Cathedral of Autun, St. Lazare, France (SCALA/Art Resource)

14: *David* (1470's), bronze statue by Andrea del Verrocchio; Bargello, Florence (Giraudon/Art Resource)

15: © Eberhard Streichan, Shostal

16: Detail of *Annunciation* (about 1490), tempera painting on panel by Botticelli; Uffizi Gallery, Florence (SCALA/Art Resource)

20: *Joseph* (about 1425), detail of Merode Altarpiece, oil painting on wood panel by Robert Campin; Metropolitan Museum of Art, the Cloister Collection, New York City

23: © Ted Gruen, Bruce Coleman Inc.

24: *Joseph and Mary in Bethlehem* (about 1560), oil on wood panel by an unknown artist; Scaiffe Gallery, Bequest of Howard A. Noble, Pittsburgh, Pennsylvania

26: *Augustus Caesar* (about 17 B.C.), marble statue by an unknown artist; Braccio Nuovo, Rome (SCALA/Art Resource)

27: © E. Otto, FPG

28: *Nativity* (about 1423), detail of the Strozzi Altarpiece, tempera on wood panel by Gentile da Fabriano; Uffizi Gallery, Florence (SCALA/Art Resource)

31: (Top) © Marvin E. Newman
(Bottom) © Shlomo Arad, Woodfin Camp, Inc.

32: Detail of *Adoration of the Shepherds* (about 1506), oil painting on wood by Giorgione; National Gallery of Art, Samuel K. Kress Collection, Washington, D.C.

35: Fred Ward, Black Star

36: © Peter Ward, Bruce Coleman Inc.

37: © Tor Eigeland, Black Star

38: Detail of *The Presentation in the Temple* (about 1660), oil painting on wood panel by Rembrandt; Mauritshuis, The Hague (SCALA/Art Resource)

42: Detail of *Adoration of the Magi* (about 1650), oil painting on canvas by Rembrandt; Göteborg Musem, Sweden

46: *Flight into Egypt* (about 1300), detail of triptych, tempera painting on wood panel with gold leaf by Duccio; Òpera del Duomo, Sienna, Italy (SCALA/Art Resource)

48: © James Hanken, Bruce Coleman Inc.

49: Detail of *Rest on the Flight to Egypt* (about 1615), an oil painting on canvas by Caravaggio; Doria Pamphily Gallery, Rome (Art Resource)

50: Detail of *Massacre of the Innocents* (about 1611), an oil painting on canvas by Guido Reni; Pinacoteca, Bologna, Italy (Art Resource)

53: (Top) © Thomas Hopker, Woodfin Camp, Inc.
(Bottom) © Marvin E. Newman

54: Detail of *Madonna of Loretto* (about 1604), an oil painting on canvas by Caravaggio; Saint Agostino, Rome (SCALA/Art Resource)

56-57: Plessner International, from FPG

59: © Barry Rosenthal, FPG

60: © Marvin E. Newman

61: © Micha Bar, Magnum

62: © Shlomo Arad, Woodfin Camp, Inc.

63: © Richard Nowitz, Black Star

64: WORLD BOOK photo by Steven Spicer